LET THERE BE CHRISTMAS

A CANTATA BY JOSEPH M. MARTIN

FULL ORCHESTRATION BY BRANT ADAMS
CONSORT ORCHESTRATION BY STAN PETHEL

Performance Time: Approx. 47 min.

(1) This symbol indicates a track number on the StudioTrax CD (accompaniment only) or SplitTrax CD.

ISBN 978-1-4950-1779-7

SHAWNEE PRESS

EXCLUSIVELY DISTRIBUTED BY

HAL•LEONARD® CORPORATION

7777 W. BLUEMOUND RD. P.O. BOX 13819 MILWAUKEE, WI 53213

Visit Hal Leonard Online at
www.halleonard.com

Visit Shawnee Press Online at
www.shawneepress.com

FOREWORD

In one great crescendo of purpose, the season of Christmas sweeps us into its arms with an unfettered flourish of festivity. The glare of this explosion of activity often overshadows the fragile light that is the spiritual center of this sacred time.

Simply, and with unexpected gentleness, Bethlehem's star flickers to life like a candle in the winter wind just when the night is longest. It kindles in the open heart a deep hope that warms and illuminates. It is by this dancing light of promise we discover the miracle of the season. Emboldened, we are drawn close to the manger. By this candle of faith we see the Child of God, wrapped in the simple, the Creator embraced and held by His own creation. It is this glorious impossible that proclaims,

Let there be SONG…as a young mother's lullaby becomes a symphony of praise that wakes the nations.

Let there be FAITH…as ancient scrolls unfurl to reveal the living Word of God.

Let there be HOPE…as the promise of a Redeemer opens like a sacred rose in the soul of the believer.

Let there be PEACE…as the Spirit descends like a Dove with healing in its wings.

Let there be LOVE…as the world feels the embrace of God's perfect light.

Let there be JOY…as our cup of worship overflows with thanksgiving.

Let there be WONDER…as each seeker's eyes reflect a glory that melts away doubt and reveals the treasure of belief.

Let there be GRACE…and discover the heart of God.

Let there be CHRISTMAS…and let the music of life begin and never end!

JOSEPH M. MARTIN

PROGRAM NOTES

LET THERE BE CHRISTMAS may be presented as a straight "stand and sing" cantata with scripture-based narration bridging the movements. If a director wishes to incorporate extra-musical elements, the notes on the following page may serve as a guide for other creative programming options. In each case, the suggested activity can be offered before, during, or immediately following the narration or anthem presentation. Placement or alteration of the activity is at the discretion of the music director or pastor. You are encouraged to adapt, alter, or add to any of these suggestions to reflect your individual worship practices and traditions.

"Christmas Overture and Processional"
The Overture is optional and the cantata may begin at measure 114.

Choirs may process if desired. The opening carol arrangement is designed to function as a "choral-only" presentation, or as a congregational participation moment. If sung with the congregation, it is recommended that the congregation stand, if able.

"The Advent Rose"
This anthem lends itself to a number of possible multi-sensory additions. Consider introducing a delicate rose incense as an enhancement to the anthem presentation. Scattering rose petals or broadcasting the incense in the traditional ways associated with liturgical worship can accomplish this.

A more subtle option would be to bring forward a white rose symbolizing faith, and place it on the altar at some point during the narration or at the close of the anthem.

"The Divine Expectation"
Light the advent candles at this point.

If this anthem is sung with the congregation, it is recommended that the congregation stand, if able.

"Concertato on O Little Town of Bethlehem"
Bring in banners inscribed with the dove symbol (representing peace). This is an opportunity for other groups (youth, children, liturgical dancers, etc.) to become involved with the presentation of the cantata. The procession of the banners into the sanctuary might lend itself to choreographed movements from these additional groups.

"Carols from a Quiet Manger"
Consider lighting candles representing Mary (light blue) and Joseph (royal blue), and a large, white candle for CHRIST. Place these candles in the center of the altar on a burlap or muslin fabric.

"Arise!"
Children may process into the sanctuary, walking quickly and waving white streamers, and surround the congregation. This is a powerful way to represent the host of angels. Use your imagination when timing this moment for maximum effect.

"Bleak Midwinter's Gift"
At this point, it is recommended that a special offering for charity or other important missions outreach be collected. This act of worship mirrors the gifts of the visiting Magi, and, once collected, can be brought forward and placed on or around the nativity gathering.

"Let There Be Christmas"
Open the church Bible and read the selected passage, and then place the Bible on a special podium and table surrounded by candles representing the Light of the world.

"A Joyful Gathering of Carols"
When presented with congregational participation, it is recommended that the congregation stand, if able.

CHRISTMAS OVERTURE
AND PROCESSIONAL *

Words by
JOHN FRANCIS WADE (1711-1786)

Incorporating tunes:
**IN DULCI JUBILO, MENDELSSOHN,
SUSSEX CAROL, SCHULZ, IL EST NÉ,
GLORIA** *and* **ADESTE FIDELES**

Arranged by
JOSEPH M. MARTIN (BMI)

* The cantata may begin at measure 114, if desired.
** Tune: IN DULCI JUBILO, traditional German melody, 14th century

LET THERE BE CHRISTMAS - SAB

* Tune: SUSSEX CAROL, traditional English melody

LET THERE BE CHRISTMAS - SAB

6

48 Moderately, with confidence (♩ = ca. 96)

* Tune: MENDELSSOHN, Felix Mendelssohn, 1809-1847

LET THERE BE CHRISTMAS - SAB

8

LET THERE BE CHRISTMAS - SAB

* For a shorter version, start at m. 114.

10

* Part for congregation is on page 96.
** Tune: ADESTE FIDELES, John Francis Wade, 1711-1786
    Words: Latin hymn, ascribed to John Francis Wade

born the King of an - gels. O come, let us a - dore Him. O

come, let us a - dore Him. O come, let us a -

dore Him, Christ the Lord.

12

LET THERE BE CHRISTMAS - SAB

NARRATION:

Let there be FAITH.

Who has believed our message, and to whom has the arm of the Lord been revealed?

For He shall grow up like a tender plant, and like a root out of parched ground; this shoot will spring from the stump of Jesse, from his roots a branch will bear much fruit. *(Isaiah 53:1-2;11:1 paraphrased)*

This is what the Lord Almighty says, "Here is My Servant whose name is 'THE BRANCH,' and from this place, He will build My church." *(Zechariah 6:12 paraphrased)*

THE ADVENT ROSE

Words by
JOSEPH M. MARTIN (BMI)

Traditional Irish Folk Song
Arranged by
JOSEPH M. MARTIN

22

softly. Peace comes gently, bring-ing mer-cy, bring-ing

grace; heav-en's blan-ket of as-sur-ance,___ warm-ing

touch___ of love's em-brace.

LET THERE BE CHRISTMAS - SAB

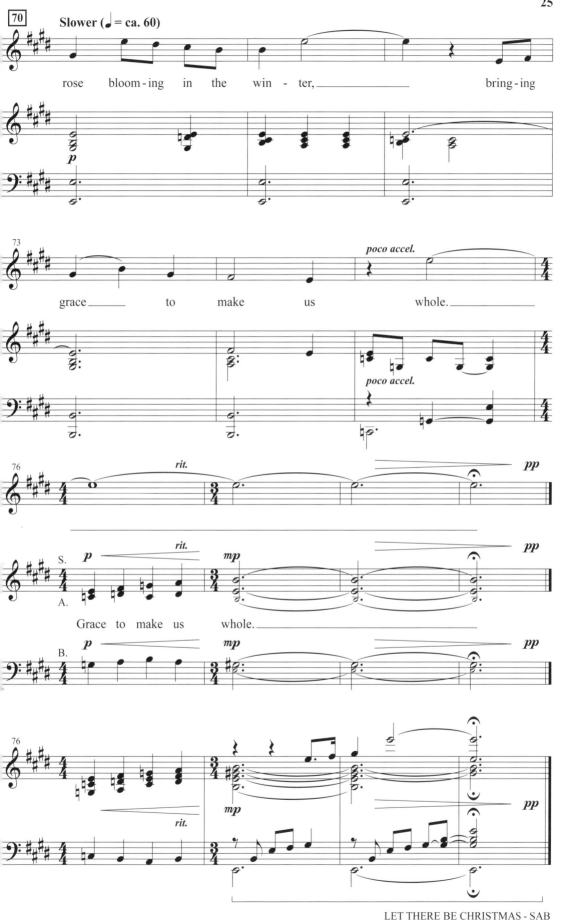

NARRATION:

Let there be HOPE.

O Israel, hope in the Lord! For with God there is steadfast love, and with Him is abundant redemption. Be strong and be of good courage, all you who wait upon the Lord! *(Psalm 130:7; 31:24 paraphrased)*

For they who wait, shall renew their strength. They shall mount up with wings like eagles. They shall run and not be weary. They shall walk and not faint. *(Isaiah 40:31 paraphrased)*

THE DIVINE EXPECTATION

Words by
CHARLES WESLEY (1707-1788)
with additional words by
JOSEPH M. MARTIN (BMI)

Based on tunes:
BRING A TORCH
Traditional French Melody
and **HYFRYDOL**
by ROWLAND H. PRICHARD (1811-1887)
Arranged by
JOSEPH M. MARTIN

LET THERE BE CHRISTMAS - SAB

28

Come, Thou long - ex - pect - ed Je - sus, born to set __ Thy peo - ple free.

From our fears __ and sins __ re-lease __ us. Let __ us find our rest in Thee. __

Come.   Come.   Come, __ Lord Je - sus. Come __ to - day.   Come.

long - ing heart.___ Come. Come. Come,_ Lord Je - sus. Come to-

day. Come. Ve - ni Em - man - u - el!

32

LET THERE BE CHRISTMAS - SAB

34

36

NARRATION:

Let there be PEACE.

Unto you, Bethlehem, though you are small among the tribes of Judah, out of you will come one who will rule over all Israel. He will stand and shepherd His flock in the strength of the Lord, in the majesty of the name of the Lord; and they will live securely, and His greatness will reach the ends of the earth. And He will be our peace. *(Micah 5:2-5 paraphrased)*

Concertato on
O LITTLE TOWN OF BETHLEHEM

Words by
PHILLIPS BROOKS (1835-1893)

Tune: **FOREST GREEN**
Traditional English Melody
Arranged by
JOSEPH M. MARTIN (BMI)

* Part for Congregation is on page 97.

LET THERE BE CHRISTMAS - SAB

hopes and fears of all __ the __ years are met in __ thee to -
prais - es sing to God __ the __ King, and peace to __ all the

night.   2. For earth!

CHOIR *only*   3. How
Sop. *p*

*(opt. a cappella)**
si - lent - ly, how si - lent - ly, the won-drous _ Gift is giv'n.   So

Oo _____

* Accompanist may double voices, if desired.

LET THERE BE CHRISTMAS - SAB

42

dear Christ_ en - ters in.

cresc. poco a poco

SOPRANOS *(a few voices)* **19** *rit.* **f**

4. O

CHOIR *and* CONGREGATION **f** *unis.*

4. O

LET THERE BE CHRISTMAS - SAB

44

NARRATION:

Let there be LOVE.

This is how the birth of Jesus Christ came about: His mother Mary was pledged to be married to Joseph; but before he knew her, she was found to be with Child through the Holy Spirit. Because Joseph was a righteous man and did not want to expose her to public disgrace, he had in mind to divorce her quietly. But after he had considered this, an angel of the Lord appeared to him in a dream and said, "Joseph, son of David, do not be afraid to take Mary home as your wife, because what is conceived in her is from the Holy Spirit. She will give birth to a Son; and you are to give Him the name Jesus, because He will save His people from their sins." All this took place to fulfill what the Lord had said through the prophet: "The virgin will be with Child and will give birth to a Son, and they will call Him Immanuel" - which means, "God with us." When Joseph woke up, he did what the angel of the Lord had commanded him and took Mary home as his wife. But he had no union with her until she gave birth to a Son. And he gave Him the name Jesus.
(Matthew 1:18-25 paraphrased)

CAROLS FROM A QUIET MANGER

Words by
JOSEPH M. MARTIN (BMI)

Based on tunes
STILL, STILL, STILL
Traditional Austrian Melody
CRUSADER'S HYMN
Schlesische Volkslieder, 1842
Arranged by
JOSEPH M. MARTIN

* Tune: STILLE NACHT, Franz Grüber, 1787-1863

see the__Child so__ still.   As   Ma - ry__ gen - tly

rocks her__ Ba - by,   an - gels_soft - ly   sing His__ prais - es.

Still,____ still,____ still,_____ come__ see the__Child so__

ho - ly star its vig - il keep - ing. Still, still,

still, can you hear the fall - ing snow?

Fair - est Lord Je - sus,

(Accompanist may double voices, if desired.)

SOPRANO SOLO

Sleep,___ sleep,___ sleep. Close Your eyes, my__ love, and

Oo_____

dream. No cry - ing__ as I gen - tly__ hold You.

52

Let my tender arms en-fold You. Sleep, sleep,

Oo

sleep. Close Your eyes, my love, and dream.

NARRATION:

Let there be JOY.

And there were shepherds, living out in the fields nearby, keeping watch over their flocks at night. An angel of the Lord appeared to them; and the glory of the Lord shone around them; and they were very terrified. But the angel said to them, "Do not be afraid. I bring you good news that will cause great joy for all the people. Today, in the town of David, a Savior has been born to you. He is the Messiah, the Lord. This will be a sign to you: You will find a Baby wrapped in cloths and lying in a manger."

Suddenly a great company of the heavenly host appeared with the angel; praising God and saying, "Glory to God in the highest heaven, and on earth peace to those on whom His favor rests." When the angels had left them and gone into heaven, the shepherds said to one another, "Let's go to Bethlehem and see this thing that has happened, which the Lord has told us about." *(Luke 2:8-15 paraphrased)*

ARISE!
(Hodie Christus natus est)

Words by
MARY FOIL
and STEPHEN MARTIN

Music by
JOSEPH M. MARTIN (BMI)

LET THERE BE CHRISTMAS - SAB

man - ger lay, has wak-ened the dawn to a glo - ri - ous day!

Ho - di - e Chri - stus na - tus est. Ho - di - e

Ho - di - e.

Chri - stus na - tus est. A -

rise, ye sleep-ers. A - wake from your rest. Come and see the Child _ who

Ho - di - e. _____

ev-er-more will bless. Through _ Him, the bat - tle of sin will be won. A -

wake from the dark-ness. Your Light now has come! Ho - di - e Chri-stus

Ho - di -

58

rise,   sleep-ers; a - wake.   Lift high your praise   this glo - ri - ous

morn.

A -

Ho - di - e._____ Come and see   the Sav - ior's

rise,   ye sleep-ers. A - wake from the night.

NARRATION:

Let there be WONDER.

Now after Jesus was born in Bethlehem of Judea, in the days of Herod the king, behold, wise men from the East came to Jerusalem, saying, "Where is He who has been born King of the Jews? For we have seen His star in the East and have come to worship Him."
(Matthew 2:1-2 NKJV*)

BLEAK MIDWINTER'S GIFT

Words by
CHRISTINA ROSSETTI (1830-1894)

Incorporating tunes:
DARKE,
SCOTTISH FOLK TUNE,
and **CRANHAM**
Arranged by
JOSEPH M. MARTIN (BMI)

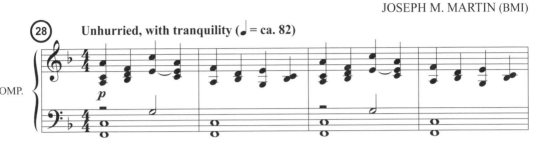

In the bleak mid-win-ter, frost-y wind made moan.

Earth stood hard as i-ron, wa-ter like a stone.

* Tune: DARKE, Harold Darke, 1888-1976

64

SOPRANO

ALTO

Heav - en can - not hold Him;

nor earth sus - tain.____ Heav'n and earth shall

flee a - way when He comes to reign.____

* Tune: Traditional Scottish melody

LET THERE BE CHRISTMAS - SAB

66

* Tune: CRANHAM, Gustav Holst, 1874-1934

LET THERE BE CHRISTMAS - SAB

NARRATION:

Let there be GRACE.

In the beginning was the Word; and the Word was with God, and the Word was God. He was in the beginning with God. All things were made through Him; and without Him was not any thing made that was made. In Him was life; and the life was the light of men. The light shines in the darkness, and the darkness has not overcome it.

The true light, which gives light to everyone, was coming into the world. He was in the world, and the world was made through Him, yet the world did not know Him. He came to His own, and His own people did not receive Him. But to all who did receive Him, who believed in His name, He gave the right to become children of God; who were born, not of blood nor of the will of the flesh nor of the will of man, but of God. *(John 1:1-5, 9-13 ESV*)*

LET THERE BE CHRISTMAS

Words and Music by
JOSEPH M. MARTIN (BMI)

SOLO (opt. all women or unison choir)

Let there be mu - sic. Let there be praise.

72

LET THERE BE CHRISTMAS - SAB

LET THERE BE CHRISTMAS - SAB

74

LET THERE BE CHRISTMAS - SAB

grace from a - bove. Christ - mas, come let our

hope be re - stored.____ Bring us news that a

Sav - ior is born! Christ, the

Heav - en has spok - en, "Let there be Light!"

Come, all ye faith - ful. Let there be Christ - mas to-

night. _____ Let there be mu - sic.

78

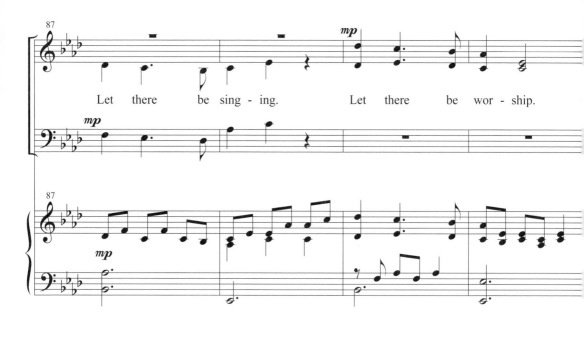

LET THERE BE CHRISTMAS - SA

NARRATION:

Let there be LIFE.

Now may the faith of the prophets,
the hope of the Scripture,
the peace of the Christ Child,
the love of His parents,
the joy of the shepherds,
the wonder of the wise men,
the grace of the season,
and the life everlasting
be yours this Christmas.
May the blessing of God Almighty,
the Father, the Son, and the Holy Spirit,
be among you and remain with you always.

A JOYFUL GATHERING OF CAROLS

Arranged by
JOSEPH M. MARTIN (BMI)

Incorporating tunes:
**REGENT SQUARE,
ANTIOCH,
W ZLOBIE LEZY,
STILLE NACHT,
THE FIRST NOEL,**
and **MENDELSSOHN**

* Tune: REGENT SQUARE, Henry T. Smart, 1813-1879

LET THERE BE CHRISTMAS - SAB

82

S.A.B. CHOIR *and* CONGREGATION*

* Part for congregation is on page 98.
** Tune: ANTIOCH, George Frederick Handel, 1685-1759; arr. Lowell Mason, 1792-1872
Words: Isaac Watts, 1674-1748

LET THERE BE CHRISTMAS - SAB

Part for congregation is on page 99.
* Tune: W ZLOBIE LEZY, traditional Polish melody
Words: traditional Polish carol

LET THERE BE CHRISTMAS - SAB

* Part for congregation is on page 100.
** Tune: STILLE NACHT, Franz Gruber, 1787-1863
   Words: Joseph Mohr, 1792-1848

LET THERE BE CHRISTMAS - SAB

89

*   Part for congregation is on page 101.
** Tune: THE FIRST NOEL, traditional English melody
    Words: traditional English carol

LET THERE BE CHRISTMAS - SAB

90

fields _____ where _ they lay _ keep - ing their sheep, on a cold win - ter's night _____ that was _____ so deep. No - el, _____ No - el, No - el, _____ No - el, _____

poco rit.

born is the King____ of Is - ra - el.

123 **Quicker, with triumphant joy** (♩ = ca. 104)

92

132 S.A.B. CHOIR *and* CONGREGATION*

**mf *unis.*

Hark! the her - ald an - gels sing,___ "Glo - ry to the new - born King; peace on earth, and mer - cy mild,___ God and sin - ners rec - on - ciled!" Joy - ful, all ye

* Part for congregation is on page 102.
** Tune: MENDELSSOHN, Felix Mendelssohn, 1809-1847
Words: Charles Wesley, 1707-1788

LET THERE BE CHRISTMAS - SAB

na - tions rise.___ Join the tri - umph of the skies.___

With th'an - gel - ic host pro - claim, "Christ is___ born in

unis.

Beth - le - hem!" Hark! the her - ald an - gels sing,

"Glo - ry___ to the new-born King!" "Glo - ry___ to the

new - born King!"

With power to the end (♩ = ca. 96)

Let there be hope! Let there be love!___

Let there be peace! Let there be

The publisher hereby grants permission to reprint the material within the box for the purpose of making performance of this cantata possible with congregational participation, provided that a sufficient quantity of copies of the entire cantata has been purchased for performance by the choir and accompanist. The music must be reproduced with the title and all credits including the copyright notice.

O COME, ALL YE FAITHFUL

Words:
JOHN FRANCIS WADE (1711-1786)

Tune: **ADESTE FIDELES**
by JOHN FRANCIS WADE
Arranged by
JOSEPH M. MARTIN (BMI)

(cong.) 1. O come, all ye faith - ful, joy - ful and tri - um - phant. O
(choir) 2. Sing, choirs of an - gels. Sing in ex - ul - ta - tion.
(cong. mel.) 3. Yea, Lord, we greet Thee; born this hap - py morn - ing.

come ye, O come ye to Beth - le - hem.
Sing all ye cit - i - zens of heav - en a - bove.
Je - sus, to Thee be all glo - ry giv'n.

Come and be - hold Him, born the King of an - gels.
Glo - ry to God; all glo - ry in the high - est. O
Word of the Fa - ther, now in flesh ap - pear - ing!

come, let us a - dore Him. O come, let us a - dore Him. O

come, let us a - dore Him, Christ the Lord.

O LITTLE TOWN OF BETHLEHEM

Words:
PHILLIPS BROOKS (1835-1893)

Tune: **FOREST GREEN**
Traditional English Melody
Arranged by
JOSEPH M. MARTIN (BMI)

The publisher hereby grants permission to reprint the material within the box for the purpose of making performance of this cantata possible with congregational participation, provided that a sufficient quantity of copies of the entire cantata has been purchased for performance by the choir and accompanist. The music must be reproduced with the title and all credits including the copyright notice.

INFANT HOLY, INFANT LOWLY

Words:
Traditional Polish Carol

Tune:
W ZLOBIE LEZY
Traditional Polish Melody
Arranged by
JOSEPH M. MARTIN (BMI)

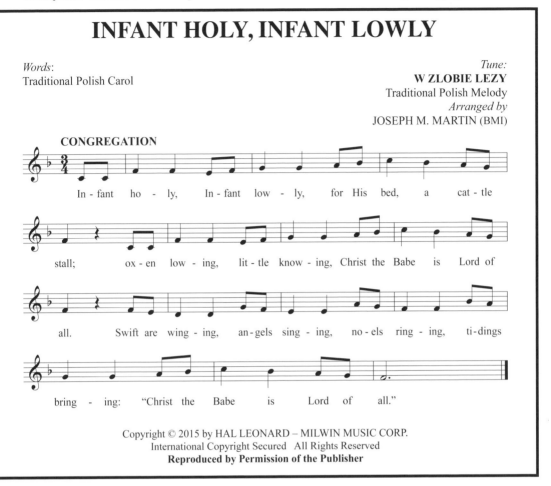

SILENT NIGHT, HOLY NIGHT!

Words:
JOSEPH MOHR (1792-1848)

Tune: **STILLE NACHT**
by FRANZ GRÜBER (1787-1863)
Arranged by
JOSEPH M. MARTIN (BMI)

The publisher hereby grants permission to reprint the material within the box for the purpose of making performance of this cantata possible with congregational participation, provided that a sufficient quantity of copies of the entire cantata has been purchased for performance by the choir and accompanist. The music must be reproduced with the title and all credits including the copyright notice.

THE FIRST NOEL

Words:
Traditional English Carol

Tune: **THE FIRST NOEL**
Traditional English Melody
Arranged by
JOSEPH M. MARTIN (BMI)

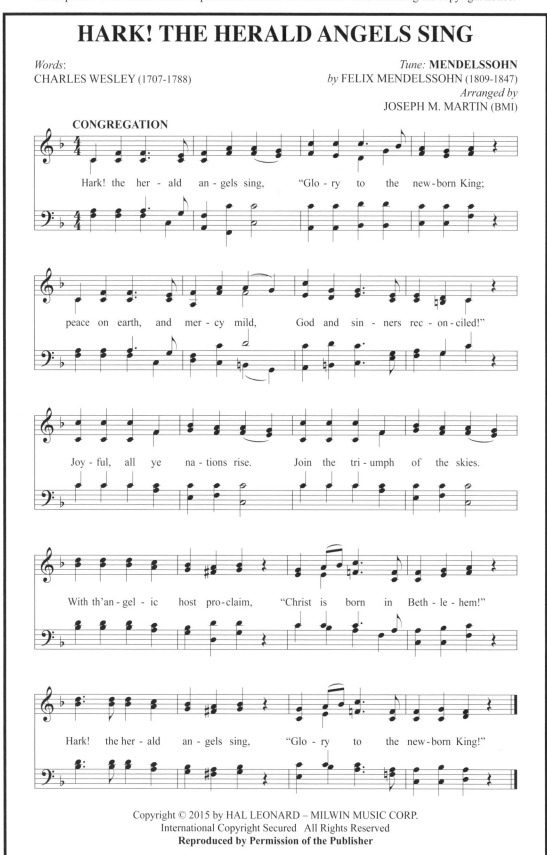

HARK! THE HERALD ANGELS SING

Words:
CHARLES WESLEY (1707-1788)

Tune: **MENDELSSOHN**
by FELIX MENDELSSOHN (1809-1847)
Arranged by
JOSEPH M. MARTIN (BMI)

CONGREGATION

Hark! the her - ald an - gels sing, "Glo - ry to the new-born King;

peace on earth, and mer - cy mild, God and sin - ners rec - on - ciled!"

Joy - ful, all ye na - tions rise. Join the tri - umph of the skies.

With th'an - gel - ic host pro-claim, "Christ is born in Beth - le - hem!"

Hark! the her - ald an - gels sing, "Glo - ry to the new-born King!"